THE BROADWAY COLLECTION

W9-DJD-397

Cover photo by Jeff Robinson

ISBN 0-634-00390-9

HAL•LEONARD® CORPORATION

7777 W. BLUEMOUND RD. P.O. BOX 13819 MILWAUKEE, WI 53213

Visit Hal Leonard Online at
www.halleonard.com

BALI HA'I
from SOUTH PACIFIC

Lyrics by OSCAR HAMMERSTEIN II
Music by RICHARD RODGERS

Grazioso

BRING HIM HOME
from LES MISÉRABLES

Music by CLAUDE-MICHEL SCHÖNBERG
Lyrics by HERBERT KRETZMER and ALAIN BOUBLIL

Moderately slow

CLIMB EV'RY MOUNTAIN
from THE SOUND OF MUSIC

Lyrics by OSCAR HAMMERSTEIN II
Music by RICHARD RODGERS

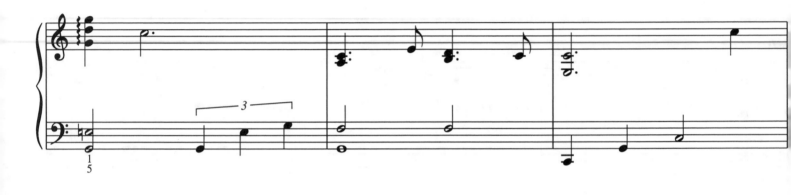

DON'T CRY FOR ME ARGENTINA

from EVITA

Words by TIM RICE
Music by ANDREW LLOYD WEBBER

Freely

Moderately slow, rhythmic

EASTER PARADE
from AS THOUSANDS CHEER

Words and Music by
IRVING BERLIN

EMPTY CHAIRS AT EMPTY TABLES
from LES MISÉRABLES

Music by CLAUDE-MICHEL SCHÖNBERG
Lyrics by HERBERT KRETZMER and ALAIN BOUBLIL

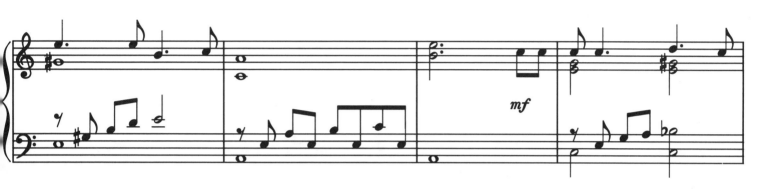

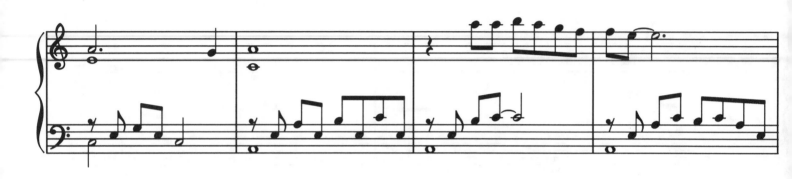

EVERYTHING'S COMING UP ROSES
from GYPSY

Words by STEPHEN SONDHEIM
Music by JULE STYNE

GETTING TO KNOW YOU
from THE KING AND I

Lyrics by OSCAR HAMMERSTEIN II
Music by RICHARD RODGERS

Gracefully

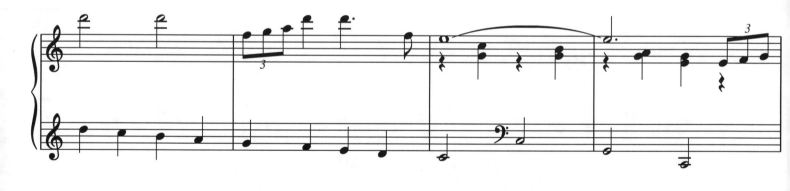

HEAT WAVE
from the Stage Production AS THOUSANDS CHEER

Words and Music by
IRVING BERLIN

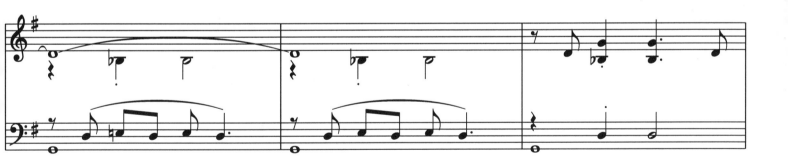

D.S. al Coda

CODA

GIGI
from GIGI

Words by ALAN JAY LERNER
Music by FREDERICK LOEWE

HOW ARE THINGS IN GLOCCA MORRA
from FINIAN'S RAINBOW

Words by E.Y. HARBURG
Music by BURTON LANE

I COULD WRITE A BOOK
from PAL JOEY

Words by LORENZ HART
Music by RICHARD RODGERS

IF I LOVED YOU
from CAROUSEL

Lyrics by OSCAR HAMMERSTEIN II
Music by RICHARD RODGERS

I DON'T KNOW HOW TO LOVE HIM

from JESUS CHRIST SUPERSTAR

Words by TIM RICE
Music by ANDREW LLOYD WEBBER

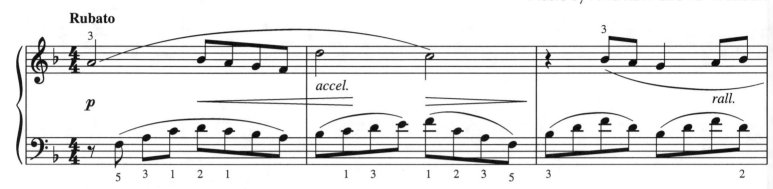

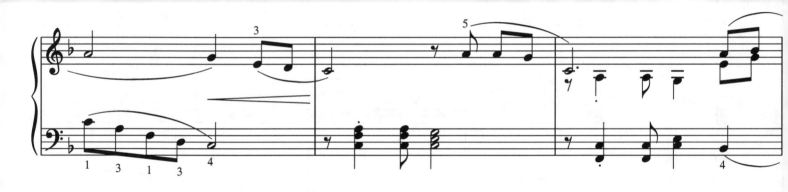

MCA Music Publishing

I'LL BE SEEING YOU

from RIGHT THIS WAY

Lyric by IRVING KAHAL
Music by SAMMY FAIN

IN MY LIFE
from LES MISÉRABLES

Music by CLAUDE-MICHEL SCHÖNBERG
Lyrics by HERBERT KRETZMER
Original Text by ALAIN BOUBLIL and JEAN-MARC NATEL

Slowly, with expression

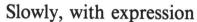

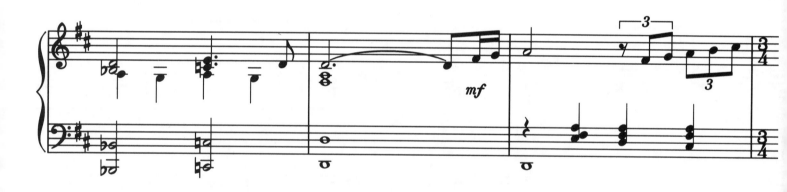

64

IT'S ALL RIGHT WITH ME
from CAN-CAN

Words and Music by
COLE PORTER

Brightly

with pedal

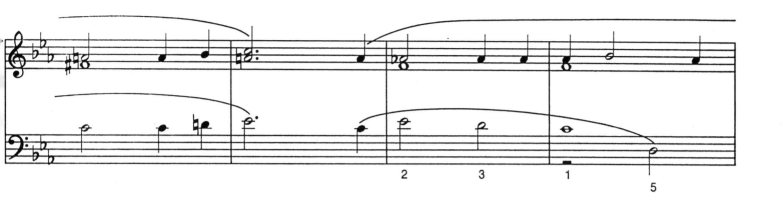

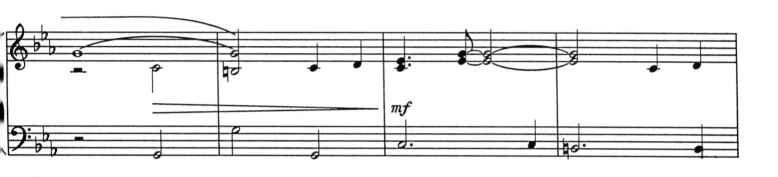

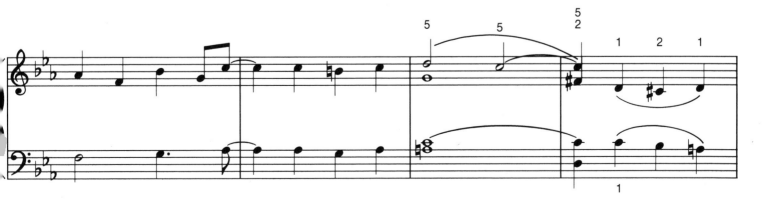

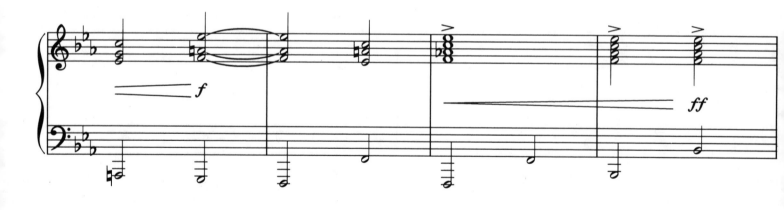

JUST IN TIME
from BELLS ARE RINGING

Words by BETTY COMDEN and ADOLPH GREEN
Music by JULE STYNE

Medium slow and swingy

Piano

THE LADY IS A TRAMP

from BABES IN ARMS

Words by LORENZ HART
Music by RICHARD RODGERS

Moderately bright Latin feel (even eighths)

Latin *(on repeat)*

THE LAST NIGHT OF THE WORLD

from MISS SAIGON

Music by CLAUDE-MICHEL SCHÖNBERG
Lyrics by RICHARD MALTBY JR. and ALAIN BOUBLIL
Adapted from original French Lyrics by ALAIN BOUBLIL

THE MUSIC OF THE NIGHT

from THE PHANTOM OF THE OPERA

Music by ANDREW LLOYD WEBBER
Lyrics by CHARLES HART
Additional Lyrics by RICHARD STILGOE

Ped. simile

rit.

p a tempo   *rit.*   *a tempo*

pp

LOVE CHANGES EVERYTHING

from ASPECTS OF LOVE

Music by ANDREW LLOYD WEBBER
Lyrics by DON BLACK and CHARLES HART

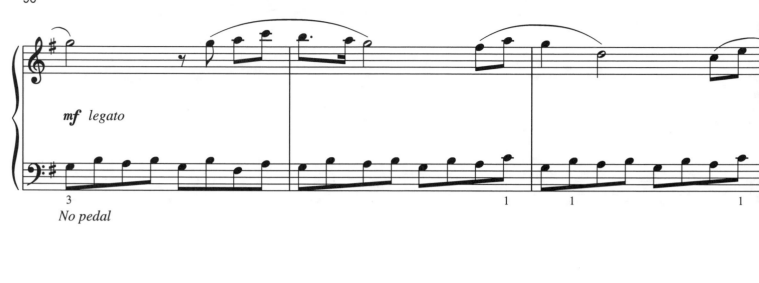

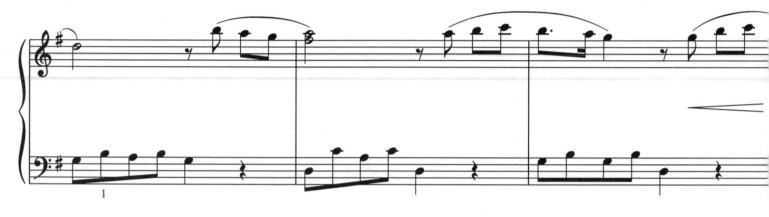

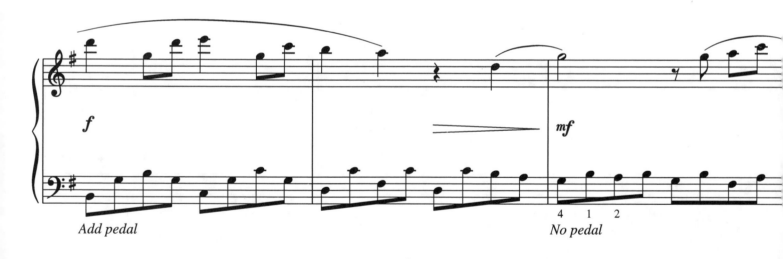

MY FUNNY VALENTINE
from BABES IN ARMS

Words by LORENZ HART
Music by RICHARD RODGERS

Slowly, poignantly

ON A CLEAR DAY
(YOU CAN SEE FOREVER)
from ON A CLEAR DAY YOU CAN SEE FOREVER

Words by ALAN JAY LERNER
Music by BURTON LANE

THE PARTY'S OVER

from BELLS ARE RINGING

Words by BETTY COMDEN and ADOLPH GREEN
Music by JULE STYNE

Largamente

PEOPLE

from FUNNY GIRL

Words by BOB MERRILL
Music by JULE STYNE

Slowly (in2)

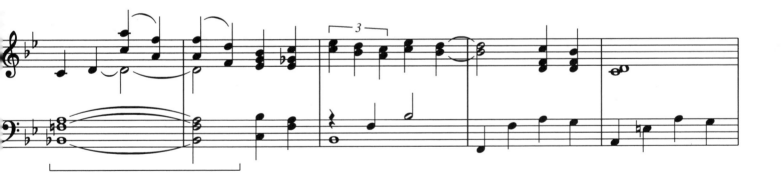

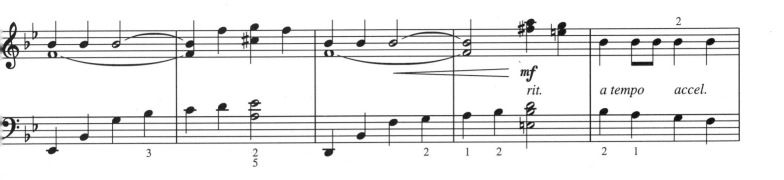

SEPTEMBER SONG
from the Musical Play KNICKERBOCKER HOLIDAY

Words by MAXWELL ANDERSON
Music by KURT WEILL

THE SURREY WITH THE FRINGE ON TOP

from OKLAHOMA!

Lyrics by OSCAR HAMMERSTEIN II
Music by RICHARD RODGERS

Moderately

with pedal

no pedal

add pedal

THIS CAN'T BE LOVE
from THE BOYS FROM SYRACUSE

Words by LORENZ HART
Music by RICHARD RODGERS

TRY TO REMEMBER

from THE FANTASTICKS

Words by TOM JONES
Music by HARVEY SCHMIDT

WHAT I DID FOR LOVE
from A CHORUS LINE

Music by MARVIN HAMLISCH
Lyric by EDWARD KLEBAN

Slowly

A WONDERFUL GUY

from SOUTH PACIFIC

Lyrics by OSCAR HAMMERSTEIN II
Music by RICHARD RODGERS

WHAT'LL I DO?
from MUSIC BOX REVUE OF 1924

Words and Music by
IRVING BERLIN

Moderate Waltz

YOUR FAVORITE MUSIC

ARRANGED FOR PIANO SOLO

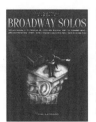

Classic Broadway Solos
16 beautifully arranged Broadway standards including: I Could Have Danced All Night • If Ever I Would Leave You • The Impossible Dream • Memory • Smoke Gets In Your Eyes • You'll Never Walk Alone • and more.

00294002 ....$10.95

Lennon & McCartney Piano Solos
22 beautiful arrangements, including: Eleanor Rigby • The Fool On The Hill • Here, There And Everywhere • Lady Madonna • Let It Be • Yesterday • and more.

00294023 ....$14.95

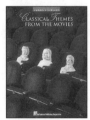

Classical Themes From The Movies
Over 30 familiar and favorite themes, including: Also Sprach Zarathustra • Ave Maria • Canon in D • Love Duet (from *La Bohème*) • Overture To *The Marriage Of Figaro* • and more.

00221010 ....$9.95

Andrew Lloyd Webber
14 pieces, including: All I Ask Of You • Don't Cry For Me Argentina • Memory • and more.

00292001.............................$12.95

Billy Joel Easy Classics
Easy Piano Solos
arranged by Phillip Keveren
preface by Billy Joel
This unique collection includes easy piano arrangements of 17 of Billy Joel's best songs: Allentown • Don't Ask Me Why • Honesty • It's Still Rock and Roll to Me • Leave a Tender Moment Alone • The Longest Time • Movin' Out (Anthony's Song) • My Life • Piano Man • Robert⁻ • She's Got a Way • Uptown Girl • more.
00306202 ....$12.95

Jazz Standards
15 all-time favorite songs, including: All The Things You Are • Bluesette • I'll Remember April • Mood Indigo • Satin Doll • and more.

00292055...........................$12.95

Love & Wedding Piano Solos

26 contemporary and classic wedding favorites, including: All I Ask Of You • Ave Maria • Endless Love • Through The Years • Vision Of Love • Sunrise, Sunset • Don't Know Much • Unchained Melody • and more.

00311507 ....$12.95

Disney's The Lion King
7 piano solos featuring: Circle Of Life • I Just Can't Wait To Be King • Be Prepared • Can You Feel The Love Tonight • and more.

00292060...........................$12.95

Movie Piano Solos
20 rich arrangements, including: The Exodus Song • The Firm Main Title • The Godfather (Love Theme) • Moon River • Raider's March • Theme From Schindler's List • When I Fall In Love • A Whole New World • and more.

00311675 ....$9.95

TV Themes
33 classic themes, including: Addams Family • Alfred Hitchcock Presents • Dinosaurs • (Meet) The Flintstones • Home Improvement • Northern Exposure • Mystery • This Is It (Bugs Bunny Theme) • Twin Peaks • and more.

00292030 ....$9.95

Narada New Age Piano Sampler
A unique collection of 17 pieces by five different artists as represented by Narada Records, one of the premier new age record labels. Artists include: David Lanz, Michael Jones, Spencer Brewer, Richard Souther, Wayne Gratz.
00490211 ....$12.95

Windham Hill Piano Sampler
This book features a sampling of ten popular Windham Hill recording artists, including: Philip Aaberg, Scott Cossu, Malcolm Dalglish, Barbara Higbie, Triona Ni Dhomhnaill, Bill Quist, Fred Simon, Ira Stein, Liz Story, and Tim Story. It is complete with biographies for each artist as well as an introduction about the Windham Hill record labels. 18 pieces in all.
00312484 ....$14.95

Sacred Inspirations
arr. Phillip Keveren
11 songs, featuring: El Shaddai • Great Is The Lord • Amazing Grace • Friends • Place In This World • and more.

00292057.............................$9.95

Piano Solos Favorites
20 arrangements, including: Born Free • Chariots Of Fire • Just The Way You Are • Unexpected Song • The Way We Were • and more.

00292068..........................$12.95

Elvis Presley Pianos Solos
A great collection of over 15 of The King's best, including: Are You Lonesome Tonight? • Don't Be Cruel • It's Now Or Never • Love Me Tender • All Shook Up • and more.

00292002.............................$9.95